Cool Filled Cupcakes

Fun & Easy Baking Recipes for Kids!

Alex Kuskowski

Checkerboard Library

An Imprint of Abdo Publishing
www.abdopublishing.com

visit us at www.abdopublishing.com

Published by Abdo Publishing, a division of ABDO,
PO Box 398166, Minneapolis, Minnesota 55439. Copyright © 2015
by Abdo Consulting Group, Inc. International copyrights reserved
in all countries. No part of this book may be reproduced in any
form without written permission from the publisher. Checkerboard
Library™ is a trademark and logo of Abdo Publishing.

Printed in the United States of America, North Mankato, Minnesota
062014
092014

Editor: Karen Latchana Kenney
Content Developer: Nancy Tuminelly
Cover and Interior Design and Production:
Colleen Dolphin, Mighty Media, Inc.
Food Production: Frankie Tuminelly
Photo Credits: Colleen Dolphin, Shutterstock

The following manufacturers/names appearing in this
book are trademarks: Betty Crocker® SuperMoist®, Dickinson's®,
Gold Medal®, Land O'Lakes®, Market Pantry®, PAM®, Pillsbury®,
Planters®, Proctor Silex®, Roundy's®, Ziploc®

Library of Congress Cataloging-in-Publication Data
Kuskowski, Alex., author.
  Cool filled cupcakes: fun & easy baking recipes for kids! /
Alex Kuskowski.
     pages cm. -- (Cool cupcakes & muffins)
  Audience: 8-12.
  Includes index.
  ISBN 978-1-62403-300-1
1. Cupcakes--Juvenile literature. I. Title.
  TX771.K87 2015
  641.8'653--dc23
                    2013043078

To Adult Helpers

Assist a budding chef by
helping your child learn to cook.
Children develop new skills, gain
confidence, and make delicious
food when they cook. Some recipes
may be more difficult than others.
Offer help and guidance to your
child when needed. Encourage
creativity with recipes. Creative
cooking encourages children to
think like real chefs.

Before getting started, have ground
rules for using the kitchen, cooking
tools, and ingredients. There
should always be adult supervision
when a sharp tool, oven, or stove is
used. Be aware of the key symbols
described on page 9. They alert
you when certain things should be
monitored.

Put on your apron. Taste their
creations. Cheer on your new chef!

Contents

For the Love of Cupcakes!

Discover the wide world of cupcakes. Cupcakes come in every size, shape, and color. Cupcakes are fun to make and eat!

Filled cupcakes are exciting to create. Every cupcake has a surprise inside. Your friends will be amazed at your cupcake creations. Try each of the recipes in this book. Or get creative and make up your own!

This book has everything you need to get started. It's filled with fun recipes. Follow each recipe's easy steps to create tasty treats. Get inspired to create cupcakes that taste and look great!

The Basics

Ask Permission

Before you cook, ask **permission** to use the kitchen, cooking tools, and ingredients. If you'd like to do something yourself, say so! Just remember to be safe. If you would like help, ask for it! Always ask when you are using a stove or oven.

Be Prepared

→ Be organized. Knowing where everything is makes cooking safer and more fun!

→ Read the directions all the way through before starting the recipe. Remember to follow the directions in order.

→ The most important ingredient is preparation! Make sure you have everything you'll need.

Be Neat and Clean

→ Start with clean hands, clean tools, and a clean work surface.

→ Tie back long hair to keep it out of the food.

→ Wear comfortable clothing and roll up your sleeves.

→ Put on an apron if you have one. It'll keep your clothes clean.

Measuring

Many ingredients are measured by the cup, tablespoon, or teaspoon. Measuring tools may come in many sizes, but the amount they measure should be printed or **etched** on the sides of the tools. When measuring 1 cup, use the measuring cup marked 1 cup and fill it to the top.

Some ingredients are measured by weight in ounces or pounds. The weight is printed on the package label.

Be Smart, Be Safe

→ Never cook if you are home alone.

→ Always have an adult nearby for hot jobs, such as ones that use the oven or the stove.

→ Have an adult around when using a sharp tool, such as a knife or a **grater**. Always be careful when using these tools!

→ Remember to turn pot handles toward the back of the stove. That way you avoid accidentally knocking the pots over.

No Germs Allowed!

Raw eggs and raw meat have bacteria in them. These bacteria are killed when the food is cooked. But bacteria can survive on things the food touched and that can make you sick! After you handle raw eggs or meat, wash your hands, tools, and work surfaces with soap and water. Keep everything clean!

Cool Cooking Terms

Here are some basic cooking terms and actions that go with them. Whenever you need a reminder, just turn back to these pages.

Wash

Always wash fruits and vegetables well. Rinse them under cold water. Pat them dry with a **towel**. Then they won't slip when you cut them.

Mix

Mix means to stir ingredients together, usually with a large spoon or electric mixer.

Whisk

Whisk means to beat quickly by hand with a whisk or a fork.

Zest

Zest means to **grate** a fruit, such as a lemon, with a zester or a grater.

Symbols

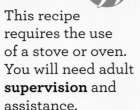

Hot!

This recipe requires the use of a stove or oven. You will need adult **supervision** and assistance.

Sharp!

This recipe includes the use of a sharp **utensil** such as a knife or **grater**. Ask an adult to help out.

Nuts!

This recipe includes nuts. Make sure to ask whether anyone you are serving has a nut allergy.

Frosting Tips

Learn the basics of frosting fun!

With frosting the possibilities are endless. You can make frosting any color and shape you want. Check out these tips to become a master chef!

Frosting the cupcake

1. Fill a plastic bag with frosting. Press out the extra air. Seal the bag closed.

2. Pinch one corner of the bag flat. Cut off the corner. You can cut it straight across, or in a V shape or M shape. This is the bag's tip.

3. Hold the bag with the tip pointed down.

4. Squeeze the bag to push out the frosting. Start on the outside edge of the cupcake. Go around the edge.

5. When you reach the beginning of the circle keep going. Make smaller and smaller circles. This creates a **spiral**.

6. Stop squeezing when finished.

V shape

M shape

straight
across

Kitchen Supplies

measuring cups

electric mixer

small heart-shaped cookie cutter

measuring spoons

mixing bowls

saucepan

scoop

muffin tin

spatula

paper liners

ice cream scoop

foil liners

plastic bags

whisk

zester

13

Ingredients

Here are some of the ingredients you will need:

chocolate
cake mix

yellow
cake mix

vanilla
cake mix

mint chocolate chip
ice cream

creamy peanut
butter

all-purpose
flour

salted roasted
peanuts

food
coloring

mini semi-sweet chocolate chips

lemon

non-stick cooking spray

mint leaves

lemon curd

strawberry jelly

chocolate pudding mix

vegetable oil

strawberries

heavy whipping cream

vanilla extract

sweetened condensed milk

Lemon Drop Cupcakes

MAKES 12 SERVINGS

Ingredients

CUPCAKES

1⅓ cups all-purpose flour
¾ tablespoon baking powder
¼ teaspoon salt
¾ tablespoon lemon zest
6 tablespoons unsalted butter, softened
1 cup white sugar
1 egg

½ teaspoon vanilla extract
½ cup buttermilk
1 cup lemon curd

FROSTING

½ cup unsalted butter, softened
1 8-oz. package cream cheese
2 cups powdered sugar
1 teaspoon vanilla extract

Tools

paper liners
muffin tin
mixing bowls
whisk
measuring cups & spoons

zester
spatula
scoop
electric mixer
plastic bag

1   **Preheat** the oven to 350 degrees. Put paper liners in the muffin tin. In a large bowl, whisk together the flour, baking powder, and salt.

2   In a medium bowl, whisk the lemon zest, butter, and sugar until **fluffy**. Mix in the egg, vanilla extract, and buttermilk. Add the butter mixture to the flour mixture. Mix well.

3   Fill the muffin cups two-thirds full of batter. Bake 16 minutes. Let the cupcakes cool.

4   Remove the cupcakes from the muffin tins. Use a teaspoon to make a hole in the top of each cupcake. Fill the holes with lemon curd.

5   Make the frosting. Put the butter and cream cheese in a medium bowl. Beat with an electric mixer until creamy. Mix in the powdered sugar and vanilla extract. Frost the cupcakes as shown on pages 10 and 11.

Mint Cream Cupcakes

Ingredients

1 18.25-oz. chocolate cake mix
1 box chocolate pudding mix
1 cup sour cream
½ cup vegetable oil
4 eggs

½ gallon mint chocolate chip ice cream
¾ cup mini semi-sweet chocolate chips
1 cup heavy whipping cream

Tools

foil liners
2 muffin tins
mixing bowl
whisk

measuring cups & spoons
scoop
small saucepan
spoon

1 **Preheat** the oven to 350 degrees. Put foil liners in the muffin tins.

2 In a large mixing bowl, whisk together the cake mix, pudding mix, sour cream, oil, eggs, and ½ cup water.

3 Put 1 tablespoon of batter in each muffin cup. Bake 8 minutes. Let the cupcakes cool 10 minutes. Then put them in the freezer for 30 minutes.

4 Scoop ice cream into the muffin cups. Fill each cup to the top. Put the cupcakes back in the freezer for 1 hour.

5 Put the heavy whipping cream in a small saucepan. Heat and stir it until it boils. Remove the pan from the heat. Stir in the chocolate chips. Let the mixture cool.

6 Put a tablespoon of chocolate mixture on each cupcake. Freeze the cupcakes for 20 minutes.

Tasty Pudding Poppers

MAKES 24 SERVINGS

Ingredients

CUPCAKES
non-stick cooking spray
1 18.25-oz. yellow cake mix
1 box vanilla pudding mix
1 cup sour cream

½ cup vegetable oil
4 eggs

FILLING
1 box vanilla pudding mix
2 cups heavy whipping cream

Tools

2 muffin tins
mixing bowls
measuring cups & spoons
whisk
scoop

sharp knife
cutting board
spatula
plastic bag

1   **Preheat** the oven to 350 degrees. Grease the muffin tins with non-stick cooking spray.

2   In a large mixing bowl, whisk together the cake mix, pudding mix, sour cream, oil, eggs, and ½ cup water.

3   Fill the muffin cups two-thirds full of batter. Bake 20 minutes. Let the cupcakes cool. Then put them in the freezer for 30 minutes.

4   In a medium bowl, whisk the filling ingredients for 5 minutes.

5   Cut the cupcakes in half **horizontally**.

6   Put a tablespoon of filling between the halves of each cupcake. Use the rest of the filling to frost the cupcakes as shown on pages 10 and 11.

21

Berry Chocolate Delight

MAKES 24 SERVINGS

Ingredients

CUPCAKES
1 18.25-oz. vanilla cake mix
1¼ cups buttermilk
⅓ cup vegetable oil
4 eggs
1 teaspoon vanilla extract

24 strawberries
mint leaves

FROSTING
1 box chocolate pudding mix
2 cups heavy whipping cream

Tools

paper liners
2 muffin tins
mixing bowls
whisk
measuring cups & spoons
scoop

electric mixer
sharp knife
cutting board
spatula
plastic bag

1 **Preheat** the oven to 350 degrees. Put paper liners in the muffin tins.

2 In a large mixing bowl, whisk together the cake mix, buttermilk, oil, eggs, and vanilla extract.

3 Fill the muffin cups three-fourths full of batter. Bake 18 to 20 minutes. Let the cupcakes cool 15 minutes.

4 Make the frosting. Put the frosting ingredients in a medium bowl. Beat with an electric mixer for 5 minutes.

5 Use a teaspoon to make a hole in the top of each cupcake. Cut the stems off of the strawberries. Put a strawberry in the hole in each cupcake.

6 Frost the cupcakes as shown on pages 10 and 11. Stick mint leaves on top of each cupcake.

23

Hidden **Heart** Cupcakes

Ingredients

CUPCAKES
non-stick cooking spray
1 18.25-oz. vanilla cake mix
1 cup buttermilk
½ cup vegetable oil
4 eggs
red food coloring

FROSTING
½ cup unsalted butter, softened
4 cups powdered sugar
1 teaspoon vanilla extract
5 tablespoons whole milk

Tools

8 x 8-inch baking pan
muffin tin
mixing bowls
measuring cups & spoons

whisk
small heart-shaped cookie cutter
electric mixer
spatula

1   **Preheat** the oven to 350 degrees. Grease the baking pan and muffin tin with non-stick cooking spray.

2   In a large mixing bowl, whisk together the cake mix, buttermilk, oil, and eggs.

3   Put one-third of the batter in a medium bowl. Mix in red food coloring. Add a few drops at a time until it's the color you want. Put the red batter in the baking pan. Bake 8 to 10 minutes. Let the cake cool. Use the cookie cutter to cut 12 heart shapes out of the cake.

4   Put 2 tablespoons of the remaining batter in each muffin cup. Put one cake heart in each cup. Press them point down into the batter. Cover each heart with 1 tablespoon of batter. Bake 15 to 18 minutes. Let the cupcakes cool.

5   Put the frosting ingredients in a medium bowl. Beat with an electric mixer until creamy. Remove the cupcakes from the muffin tins. Use a spatula to frost the cupcakes.

Cookie Dough Surprise

MAKES 24 SERVINGS

Ingredients

FILLING

4 tablespoons unsalted butter, softened
6 tablespoons brown sugar
1 cup all-purpose flour
1 7-oz. can sweetened condensed milk
¼ teaspoon vanilla extract
¼ cup mini semi-sweet chocolate chips

CUPCAKES

1 18.25-oz. chocolate cake mix
1 cup buttermilk

½ cup vegetable oil
3 eggs
1 teaspoon vanilla extract

FROSTING

½ cup unsalted butter, softened
4 cups powdered sugar
5 tablespoons milk
2 teaspoons vanilla extract
¼ cup mini semi-sweet chocolate chips

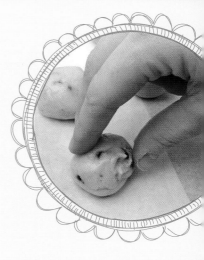

Tools

measuring cups & spoons
mixing bowls
spatula
baking sheet

paper liners
2 muffin tins
whisk

1. Mix all of the filling ingredients together in a medium mixing bowl. Form the dough into 1-inch balls and place them on a baking sheet. Put them in the freezer for 2 hours.

2. **Preheat** the oven to 350 degrees. Put paper liners in the muffin tins.

3. In a large bowl, whisk together the cake mix, buttermilk, oil, eggs and vanilla extract. Fill the muffin cups two-thirds full of batter. Place a cookie dough ball in the center of each cup. Bake 17 minutes. Let the cupcakes cool.

4. Make the frosting. In a medium bowl, whisk the butter and sugar until creamy. Mix in the milk and vanilla extract. Remove the cupcakes from the muffin tins. Use a spatula to frost the cupcakes. Top with chocolate chips.

Jelly 'n' Peanut Butter Pops

Ingredients

CUPCAKES

1⅓ cups all-purpose flour
¼ teaspoon baking soda
¾ teaspoon baking powder
¼ teaspoon salt
¾ cup unsalted butter, softened
1⅓ cups white sugar
⅓ cup creamy peanut butter
3 eggs
1 teaspoon vanilla extract

½ cup sour cream
½ cup of chopped salted
   roasted peanuts
½ cup strawberry jelly

FROSTING

½ cup unsalted butter, softened
1 cup creamy peanut butter
3 tablespoons whole milk
2 cups powdered sugar

Tools

paper liners
2 muffin tins
mixing bowls
whisk
measuring cups & spoons

scoop
spoon
electric mixer
spatula
plastic bag

1   **Preheat** the oven to 375 degrees. Put paper liners in the muffin tins. In a large mixing bowl, whisk together the flour, baking soda, baking powder, and salt.

2   Put the butter and sugar in a medium bowl. Mix with an electric mixer. Mix in the peanut butter, eggs, and vanilla extract. Add the peanut butter mixture to the flour mixture. Mix for 5 minutes. Mix in the sour cream and peanuts.

3   Fill the muffin cups one-third full of batter. Put a spoonful of jelly in the center of each cup. Cover the jelly with a small scoop of batter. Bake 20 minutes or until the cupcakes turn light brown. Let the cupcakes cool.

4   Make the frosting. Put the butter and peanut butter in a medium bowl. Mix with an electric mixer. Mix in the milk and sugar. Remove the cupcakes from the muffin tins. Frost the cupcakes as shown on pages 10 and 11.

Conclusion

Filled cupcakes have a surprise inside every one.
Making filled cupcakes doesn't have to be hard.
It can be easy and fun!

This book has tons of fun recipes to get you started.
There's more to discover too. Check your local
library for more cupcake cookbooks. Or use your
imagination and whip up your very own creations!

You can make cupcakes for birthdays, holidays, or
just for fun. Your friends and family will love tasting
your sweet creations. Become a muffin tin chef today!

Web Sites

To learn more about cool cooking, visit ABDO online at
www.abdopublishing.com. Web sites about cool cooking
are featured on our Book Links page. These links are
monitored and updated to provide the most current
information available.

Glossary

etch – to carve into something.

fluffy – light, soft, and airy.

grate – to shred by rubbing on something rough or sharp, such as a grater or zester.

horizontally – in the same direction as the ground, or side-to-side.

permission – when a person in charge says it's okay to do something.

preheat – to heat an oven to a certain temperature before putting in the food.

spiral – a pattern that winds in a circle.

supervision – the act of watching over or directing others.

towel – a cloth or paper used for cleaning or drying.

utensil – a tool used to prepare or eat food.

Index